WALKING LIKE THE PROF

WRITTEN BY MOIN UDDIN KHAN
ILLUSTRATED BY KAMRUL HUSSAIN

WALKING
LIKE THE
PROPHET

Published by IDEA Press
Copyright © IDEA Press 2015
ISBN 978-0-9929736-2-9
A Project of SHADE

Proceeds generated from the sales of these publications will go towards SHADE which is a UK registered charity.

To purchase 'Just Like The Prophet' series and other publications please contact:

w: alrawda.org
e: info@alrawda.org
t: +44 (0) 20 7998 7768

Author's Note

All praise to Allah Lord of the worlds and salutations upon His Messenger Muhammad ﷺ.

This book teaches the Sunnah practices of the Prophet Muhammad ﷺ in his day to day life, from how he would greet people to how he would walk and the things he would say in the various scenario that we can follow and implement into our lives today. It mentions over 40 etiquette in sequence and in simple rhyming English.

This endeavour was to provide an alternative to the common nursery rhymes and to help develop an Islamic identity. Every line has at least one Sunnah backed by a verse of the Holy Qur'an or Hadith. Even though it's aimed towards children, adults can also benefit by the rhyming easy to remember lines.

An immense amount of effort has been made to bring this project to this stage. We would like to thank all those who have supported us with their time, effort and funds.

Whatever is correct of this work is from Allah and His Messenger.ﷺ Whatever mistakes therein is from myself and Shaytan.

Moin Uddin Khan
(a humble servant in need of Allah)
London, UK
Rabi ul Awwal 1437 / December 2015

Dedicated to my beloved brothers and sisters across the Muslim Ummah, especially those who are being oppressed due to their faith.

Allah almighty made humans in perfect form,
He made Muhammad ﷺ the best to be born,
from his life there are inspirations to be drawn,
we should follow him in the way he has shown.

1

He was first to offer Salam,
to whomsoever he would meet.

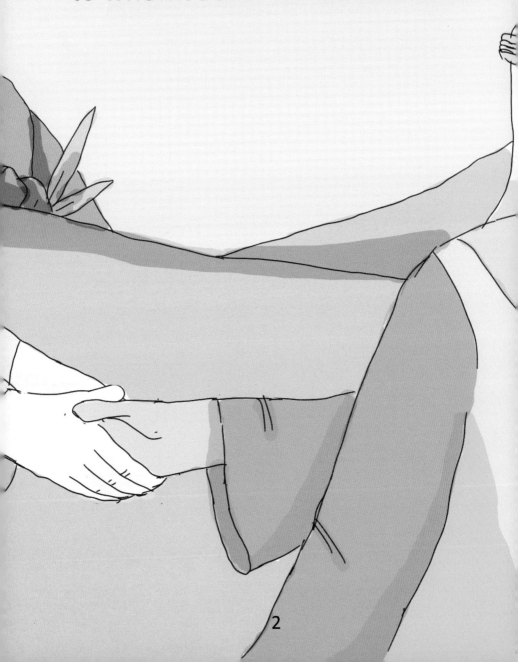

With a smile on his face,
everyone he would greet.

He would not look around,
when walking in the street.

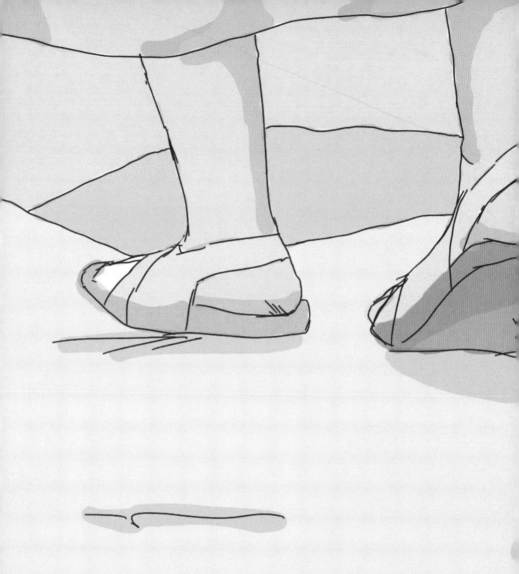

He would look at the ground,
where he placed his feet.

His legs would move fast, as if
coming down from a high place.

Keeping up with him was hard,
yet his walk was a normal pace.

If someone called him, he would turn with his whole body & his face.

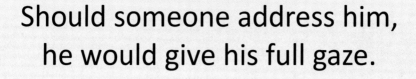

Should someone address him,
he would give his full gaze.

He would start with the right foot
when wearing his shoes.

He would begin with the left,
when it was time to remove.

He would use his right foot first,
whilst climbing onto his ride.

He would say
"Glory to Allah who gave us control
over it, we were unable otherwise".

Horse-riding and swimming
were activities he would advise.

He had a passion for archery
and would race with his wife.

He would keep a walking stick,
when going out of town.

If he prayed outdoors, he would
plant it into the ground.

17

He would remove harmful objects lying on the road.

He would help elderly people
carry their load.

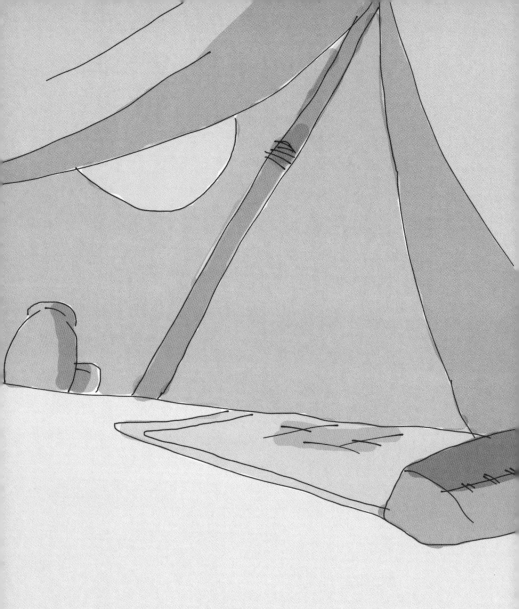

He would go around visiting
people, who had been taken ill.

He would say *"Don't worry;*
it will be a purification if Allah wills".

When going to the bathroom,
he would use his left foot to go in.

Saying *"my lord, I seek refuge in you, from the male and female Jinn"*.

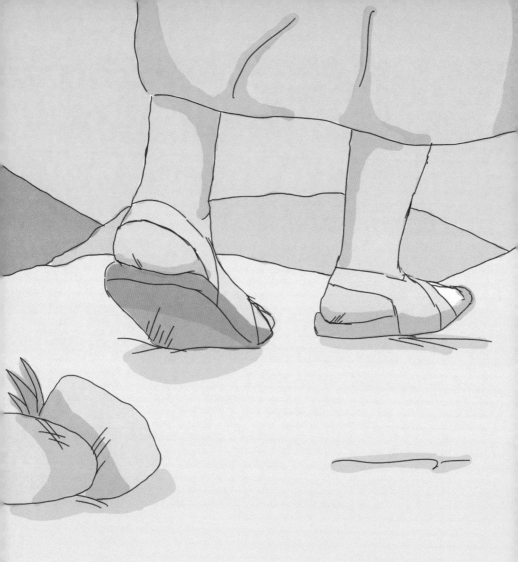

He would exit with his right foot,
Allah's pardon he would beseech.

He would say
*"Praise to Allah who relieved me of
this burden and gave me ease"*.

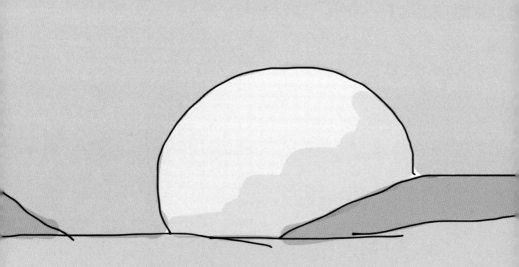

Leaving the house he would say "with Allah's name, I place my trust in him."

"There is no power or might beside
him, the most high, the supreme.

He would be kind to his neighbours, and would keep ties with his kin.

He would visit the graves,
and seek forgiveness for their sins.

He would weep for his nation and for his brothers who haven't seen him.

May Allah allow us to drink from his hand, when we meet him at his spring.

We pray that we follow his path to
paradise,and meet him therein.
Amin.

Easy Memorisation

He was first to offer Salam, to whomsoever he would meet.

With a smile on his face, everyone he would greet.

He would not look around, when walking in the street.

He would look at the ground, where he placed his feet.

His legs would move fast, as if coming down from a high place.

Keeping up with him was hard, yet his walk was a normal pace.

If someone called him, he would turn his whole body & his face.

Should someone address him, he would give his full gaze.

He would start with the right foot when wearing his shoes.

He would begin with the left when it was time to remove.

He would use his right foot first, whilst climbing onto his ride.

"Glory to Allah who gave us control over it, we were unable otherwise.

Horse-riding & swimming, were activities he would advise.

He had a passion for archery & would race with his wife.

He would keep a walking stick, when going out of town.

If he prayed outdoors, he would plant it into the ground.

He would remove harmful objects lying on the road.

He would help elderly people carry their load.

He would go around visiting people, who had been taken ill.

He would say "Don't worry; it will be a purification if Allah wills".

When going to the bathroom, he would use his left foot to go in.

Saying "my lord I seek refuge in you, from the male and female Jinn".

He would exit with his right foot, Allah's pardon he would beseech.

"Praise to Allah who relieved me of this burden and gave me ease".

Leaving the house he would say "with Allah's name, I place my trust in him."

"There is no power or might beside him, the most high, the supreme."

He would be kind to his neighbours, & would keep ties with his kin.

He would visit the graves, & seek forgiveness for their sins.

He would weep for his nation & for his brothers who haven't seen him.

May Allah allow us to drink from him, when we meet him at his spring.

'This book is the third publication of the
'Just Like The Prophet Series'

Other books by the author
Life of Muhammad The Sublime: Biography Simply Told in Poetic Rhyme

About SHADE

SHADE is a UK based charitable umbrella organisation, which endeavours to help society tackle many of the challenges it faces. SHADE runs various projects and activities for the community at large, its programmes engage people from all walks of life and brings them together to encourage respect, understanding and tolerance. It has five different sectors in which there are projects dealing with different aspects of an individual's needs. This has been divided into five sectors: Social, Health, Aid, Development & Education.

Support Us

Visit: www.alrawda.org/donate

Phone: 020 7998 7768

Bank Transfer:
HSBC Bank
a/c: 12030748
s/c: 40-02-34

UK Charity No. 1149699

The Shade Centre
Unit 1, Church Rd Studios
62 Church Road, London E12 6AF
W: www.theshade.org | E: info@theshade.org